# Prayers for Daily Strength

### Praying for the Answer NOT the Problem!

## Ivy Caddell

**PriorityONE**
*publications*
**Detroit, MI USA**

Prayers for Daily Strength: Praying for the Answer NOT the Problem!
Copyright © 2013 Ivy Caddell

Unless otherwise annotated all Scripture quotations are taken from the HOLY BIBLE, KING JAMES VERSION (Authorized).

Scripture quotations marked (NIV) are taken from the HOLY BIBLE, NEW INTERNATIONAL VERSION®. NIV®. Copyright© 1973, 1978, 1984 by International Bible Society. Used by permission of Zondervan. All rights reserved.

All rights reserved. No part of this publication may be reproduced, stored in a retrieval system, or transmitted in any form or by any means – electronic, mechanical, photocopy, recording, or any other – except for brief quotations in printed reviews, without the prior permission of the publisher.

PriorityONE Publications
P. O. Box 34722 / Detroit, MI 48234
E-mail: info@priorityonebooks.com
URL: http://www.priorityonebooks.com

ISBN 13:   978-1-933972-36-7
ISBN 10:       1-933972-36-X

*Interior, Cover Design and Editing by Christina Dixon*

Printed in the United States of America

# Table of Contents

*Acknowledgements* ................................................................. *5*
*Introduction* ........................................................................... *7*
*How to Have an Effective Prayer Life* ................................. *9*
*Protection* ............................................................................. *10*
*May I Find Work with God All Things Are Possible* ............ *11*
*How to Overcome Satan* ...................................................... *12*
*How Faith Comes* ................................................................. *13*
*Control Your Tongue* ............................................................ *14*
*I Seek Help with My Money Problems* ................................ *15*
*If Your Have a Financial Need* ............................................ *16*
*Gospel Pills* ........................................................................... *17*
*I'm Grateful Lord* .................................................................. *18*
*Stress* ..................................................................................... *19*
*Proverb* .................................................................................. *20*
*Don't Quit* ............................................................................. *21*
*Trust and Believe* ................................................................. *22*
*The Joy of the Lord* .............................................................. *23*
*A Vehicle to Meet My Needs* ............................................... *24*
*Oh Lord Please Keep This Child from Bad Friends* ............ *25*
*I Pray that My Child Does Better in School* ....................... *27*
*He Will Hear* ........................................................................ *28*

*Deliver Me from My Leg Problems and
    Take Away from Me All Sickness* ................................... 29
*Confession of Healing* ............................................................ 30
*I Want to be Relieved from Arthritis* ......................................... 32
*Prayer for Overweight* ............................................................ 33
*Prayer for High Blood Pressure* ............................................... 34
*A Prayer for Deliverance from Lupus* ....................................... 35
*A Prayer for Deliverance from Sickle Cell Anemia* ................. 36
*A Prayer for Deliverance from
    Post Traumatic Stress Disorder* ....................................... 38
*Praying the Word of God* ........................................................ 39
*What are the Signs of the End?* ............................................... 43

## Acknowledgments

I give my love and thanks to a number of special people who have contributed to this mission.

To my husband, Tom Caddell Jr., to my mother, Mary Dykes; thanks to the Dykes and Caddell families.

Thanks to my faithful friends Valdina M. Wiley, to Evangelist Ethel M. Brantley, on whom I rely.

Thanks also to Pastor Witherspoon, to the Messias Temple Church family, and thanks to Evangelist Cheryl Bass Foster.

# Introduction

As a "Faith and Prayer Warrior" I have been inspired to write, "Prayers for Daily Strength," after acknowledging the need for people to learn how to pray for the answer and not the problem.

My vision of writing this book began during my junior high school years. My sister ordered a magazine entitled "Faith," and it talked about how to take the word of God and apply it to your everyday life. My sister actually started the early writings of this book and now the Lord has blessed me to complete it.

Coming from many circumstances in life, which I could not have survived without prayer, the word of God imbedded in my heart. God's word has continuously lived within me and along with a consistent prayer life has made me whole. I would not have survived without it. God's word is real. It is true, life has sustained me and it can sustain you as well. God has blessed me abundantly above all that I could ask or think. I am a loving wife, mother, grandmother, sister, friend, servant of the Lord in prison, prayer and radio ministries, a college graduate, a true lover of life, people, animals and a faithful member of Messias Temple Church, Ypsilanti, MI. under the pastorate of Bishop Harry S. Grayson.

I admonish you to take time to read this book. You must know and understand that God's Word is life. John 1:1 states that "In the beginning was the Word, and the Word was with God, and the Word was God." I cannot stress enough the importance and the necessity to not just read your Bible, but you must study it and let the Word of God saturate your mind, soul, spirit and heart. Along with the Word of God you must have a strong and consistent prayer life; a private time for you to communicate directly with Him. I Thessalonians 5:17 states; "Pray without ceasing." The two together is what is necessary to get to know God, and to know when He is speaking, and to also build a close and personal relationship with Him.

In conclusion, I John 5:15 states: "And if we know that He hears us, whatsoever we ask, we know that we have the petitions that we desired of Him."

# How to Have an Effective Prayer Life

Father, in the name of Jesus, I thank You that You watch over Your Word to perform it, and that we can pray the Word.

> Be careful for nothing, but in everything by prayer and supplication with thanksgiving let your request be made known unto God. And the peace of God which passeth all understanding shall keep your hearts and minds through Christ Jesus.
> Philippians 4:6-7

> Verily I say unto you, Whatsoever ye shall bind on earth shall be bound in heaven: and whatsoever ye shall loose on earth shall be loosed in heaven. Again I say unto you, that if the two of you shall agree on earth as touching any thing that they shall ask, it shall be for them of my Father which is in heaven. Matthew 18:18-19

> Ask, and it shall be I given you; seek, and ye shall find; knock, and it shall be opened unto you.
> Matthew 7:7

> For the eyes of the Lord are upon the righteous, and his ears are open unto their cry. Psalm 34:15

> I cried unto the Lord with my voice; evening and morning and at noon, will I pray, and cry aloud: and he shall hear my voice. Psalm 55:17

# Protection

Father, You are my Helper, put Your arm around me.

> He that dwelleth in the secret place of the most High shall abide under the shadow of the Almighty. I will say of the Lord, He is my refuge and my fortress: My God; in Him will I trust. Surely he shall deliver thee from the snare of the fowler, and from the noisome pestilence. He shall cover thee with his feathers, and under His wings shalt thou trust. His truth (the word) shall be thy shield and buckler. A thousand shall fall at thy side and ten thousand at thy right hand, but it shall not come nigh thee. For He shall give His angels charge over thee to keep thee in all thy ways. Psalm 91

Father protect me and my loved ones from all of the crime and cruelty in this world today: and I will walk a safe path, and let us be thankful always in Jesus' name.

# May I Find Work?
## With God All Things Are Possible

    Dearest Lord I seek You, with all my heart every day of my life. I turn to You for so much and accept the deep thankfulness that flows from my soul for all Your merciful blessings. Yes, there is something special that I would like for You to make possible for me; <u>which is a good job.</u>

    Open Your door wide to prosperity and bless me in my efforts. Brighten my path, so that I may find a decent and good job, which I desperately need. Grant that I may be allowed to earn adequate wages enough to make difficulties easier, burdens lighter, and joys sweeter. Guide me and fill me with trust in Your wisdom. Amen.

# How to Overcome Satan

Finally, my brethren, be strong in the Lord, and in the power of his might. Put on the whole armor of God that ye may be able to stand against the wiles of the devil.

And take the helmet of salvation, and the sword of the spirit, which is in the word of God.

Submit yourselves therefore to God. Resist the devil, and he will flee from you.

And He said unto them, I beheld Satan as lightning fall from heaven.

Behold, I give unto you power to tread on serpents and scorpions, and over all the power of the enemy: and nothing shall by any means hurt you.

                Ephesians 6:10-17, James 4:7-8, Luke 10:18-19

# How Faith Comes

But without faith it is impossible to please Him: For he that cometh to God must believe that He is, and that He is a rewarder of them that diligently seek Him.

So then faith cometh by hearing and hearing by the word of God. If we don't have faith, it is not God's fault. To blame God for our lack of faith is nothing but ignorance. God has provided the way whereby everyone can have faith.

If any of you lack wisdom, let him ask of God, that giveth to all men liberally and upbraideth not and it shall be given Him.

But let him ask in faith, nothing wavering. For he that wavereth is like a wave of the sea driven with the wind and tossed. For let not that man think that he shall receive anything of the Lord. A double-minded man is unstable in all his ways.

For we walk by faith, not by sight.

Read: Hebrews 11:3, Romans 10:17, James 1:5-8, II Corinthians.5:7

# Control Your Tongue

Father, we come together in prayer now to seek control of our tongue.

> "He that keepeth his mouth keepeth his life: but he that openeth wide his lips shall have destruction." Proverbs 13:3

> "Whosoever keepeth his mouth and his tongue, keepeth his soul from troubles." Proverbs 21:23

> "Death and life are in the power of the tongue: and they that love it shall eat the fruit thereof."
> Proverbs 18:21

> "A wholesome tongue is a tree of life, but perverseness therein is a breach in the spirit."
> Proverbs 15:4

> "The lip of truth shall be established for ever: but a lying tongue is but for a moment." Proverbs 12:19

> "Set a watch, O Lord, before my mouth; keep the door of my lips." Psalms 141:3

Father keep us together in warm and loving bonds, so that we may speak to You in one loving voice forever. Amen.

# I Seek Help with My Money Problems

Father, it is so good to meet with thee in prayer for all matters, giving us the opportunity of *"Casting all your care upon him; for he careth for you."* 1 Peter 5:7

I have no doubt Father, that with You all things are possible; and so it is that I have great hope in asking for a special blessing. Father, I am so concerned about my money problems and my bills. It takes so much money to live these days with my income; it is very hard to make ends meet.

I pray that You will give me the wisdom to manage every penny more wisely. Help me also to overcome the temptation to buy things I really do not need so that I may get out of debt and stay out.

I know it is Your will that I should honestly and rightfully have money to cover my living expenses. I trust You to guide me, for I know You care for me.

In Jesus' name.

# If You Have a Financial Need

Father, in the name of Jesus, Your Word says that You will supply all my need according to Your riches in glory by Christ Jesus.

Your Word says that whatsoever things I desire when I pray to believe that I receive them. Therefore, I believe that my needs are supplied according to Your riches in glory by Christ Jesus.

I have given. Therefore, it is given to me -- good measure, pressed down, shaken together and running over. I have abundance and there is no lack. I sow bountifully, therefore, I reap bountifully.

Father, You make all grace abound toward me and I, having all sufficiency in all things, do abound to every good work. For the Lord is my Shepherd and I do not want.

# Gospel Pills

For poverty He has given me wealth, for sickness He has given me health, for death He has given me eternal life.
 II Corinthians 8:9; Isaiah 53:5-6; John 10:10; John 5:24

I am a member of the Body of Christ. I am redeemed from the curse for Jesus bore my sicknesses and carried my diseases in His own body. By His stripes I am healed. I forbid any sickness or disease to operate in my body. Every organ, every tissue of my body functions in the perfection in which God created it to function. I honor God and bring glory to Him in my body.
 Galatians 3:13; Matthew 8:17; I Peter 2:24; I Corinthians 6:20

## I'm Grateful Lord

Words of thanks I do pray,
Thanks for guidance each day,
Thanks for keeping me aright,
Thanks for each quiet night.
Thanks for easing any fear,
Thanks for being ever near,
Thanks for love you do share,
Thanks for your eternal care!

# Stress

Father, Who has great and abiding love for each one of Your children, I ask You now to bless with healing from stress, as I believe Your Word.

> Casting all your cares upon him; for he careth for you. 1 Peter 5:7

> He restoreth my soul; he leadeth me in the paths of righteousness for his name sake. Yea, though I walk through the valley of the shadow of death, I will fear no evil: For thou art with me; thy rod and thy staff they comfort me. Psalm 23:3-4

> Fear thou not; for I am with thee: be not dismayed; for I am thy God: I will strengthen thee; yea, I will help thee; yea, I will uphold thee with the right hand of my righteousness. Isaiah 41:10

> Peace I leave with you, my peace I give unto you; not as the world giveth, give I unto you. Let not your heart be troubled neither let it be afraid. John 14:27

Thank You for hearing my prayer Father. Thank You for the peace I feel in my heart and mind as I kneel before Your throne of Grace. In Jesus' name.

## Proverb

Risk taking is the stuff
that makes empires
and individuals grow.

Making changes
in our lives
is risky business.

But not taking chances
is the greatest risk of all!

# Don't Quit
## by John Greenleaf Whittier

When things go wrong, as they sometimes will,
When the road you're trudging seems all uphill,
When the funds are low and the debts are high,
And you want to smile, but you have to sigh,
When care is pressing you down a bit --
Rest if you must, but don't you quit.
Life is queer with its twists and turns,
As every one of us sometimes learns,
And many a failure turns about
When he might have won had he stuck it out.
Don't give up though the pace seems slow --
You may succeed with another blow.
Often the goal is nearer than
It seems to a faint and faltering man;
Often the struggler has given up
When he might have captured the victor's cup;
And he learned too late when the night slipped down,
How close he was to the golden crown.
Success is failure turned inside out --
The silver tint of the clouds of doubt,
And you never can tell how close you are,
It may be near when it seems afar;
So stick to the fight when you're hardest hit -
It's when things seem worst that you must not quit!
For all the sad words of tongue or pen,
The saddest are these: "It might have been!"

# Trust and Believe

Whatever our problems, troubles, and sorrows
If we trust in the Lord,
There'll be brighter tomorrows.
For there's nothing too hard
For the great God to do,

And all that He asks or expects from you…

Is faith that's unshaken by tribulations and tears
That keeps growing stronger along with the years,
Content in the knowledge that God knows best
And that trouble and sorrow are only a test
For without God's testing of our soul
It never would reach its ultimate goal…

Just keep on believing, whatever betide you,
Knowing that God will be with you to guide you,
And all that He promised will be yours to receive
If you trust Him completely and always believe. Amen.

# The Joy of the Lord

Father, I seek You, with all my heart everyday of life. I turn to You for so much love. But let all those that trust in You rejoice: let them ever shout for joy, because You defend them: let them also that love Your name be joyful in You (Psalm 5:11).

You said all that labor and are heavy laden could come to You and You would give them rest (Matthew 11:28). I will praise thee, O Lord, with my whole heart; I will show forth all thy marvelous works. I will be glad and rejoice in thee; I will sing praise to thy name, O thou most High. (Psalm 9:1-2)

Make my faith a little stronger; make my trust a little greater, make my love a little brighter. Amen.

# A Vehicle to Meet My Needs

Father, I thank You so much for really caring about my life through each blessing You send me. I draw close to You now in prayer, to let You know something that's very important to me. I humbly ask You to bless me with a car to meet my needs.

For often it's difficult to travel from place to place without a means of transportation I can call my own. Jesus lead me to find a good car which will serve my needs; and may it be a fair price that I can afford to pay; for things are so costly in this day and age, and I would like to stay within my budget.

I trust in You to do what's right for me always, please give me the wisdom to know when, where and how to get the vehicle I long to own. I pray that it will be soon, because You said *"Whatsoever ye shall ask in prayer, believing, ye shall receive."* (Matthew 21:22)

In the name of Jesus.

# O Lord Please Keep This Child from Bad Friends

*"He shall be their shepherd."* Ezekiel 34:23

Dear Lord, I thank You for the blessing You have showered upon me and for the faith that sustains me. The gift of prayer brightens each day, for when I can talk with You I feel so peaceful, so ready to cope with daily living. There is nothing too hard for You.

Hear me, O Lord, for I am concerned about my child who is dear to me. I want only the best for this youngster: health, education, a long and happy life, and the comfort of true faith. And I am sure my dear one is a good child, one who does not seek trouble or do terrible things. But it is hard to encourage the right kind of behavior when there are so many people around to set a poor example. I worry that this child will fall into the company of bad friends and go astray.

Your Word instructs me that your covenant extends to my offspring:

> "As for me, this is my covenant with them," says the Lord. "My Spirit, who is on you, will not depart from you, and my words that I have put in your mouth will always be on your lips, on the lips of your children, and on the lips of their descendants– from this time on and forever," says the Lord.
>
> Isaiah 59:21 NIV

Please guide me in how I can best help my loved one grow up safe and happy! I know I can't always be around when someone says "try this." So please, dear Lord, protect this child from harm as I continue to raise them up as You have instructed me, I pray Your Word over my child in the following prayer.

___*(insert your child's name here)*___ forget not my law, but let your heart keep my commandments, for length of days and long life, and peace, shall be added to you.

Trust in the Lord with all your heart; and lean not to your own understanding. Attend to my word; incline thine ear unto my sayings. Let them not depart from your eyes; keep them in the midst of your heart.

___*(insert your child's name here)*___ will lift up his/her eyes unto the hills, from whence comes his/her help which comes from the Lord. The Lord which made heaven and earth. I cried with my whole heart; for great is God's mercy toward ___*(insert your child's name here)*___. The Lord has delivered your soul. May you praise the Lord your God with all your heart; and glorify His name forever more. Amen.

Proverbs 3:1-2, 5; 4:20-21; Psalm 121:1-2; Psalm 119:145a, Psalm 86:12-13

# I Pray that My Child Does Better in School

    Father one of my concerns now, O Lord is a child who is close to me. I know this young one should be doing better in school, but I don't know how I can help. These days it is very important to get an education, without schooling there just aren't many jobs, and people can't make a good life for themselves. I don't know why my dear one is doing so poorly, but I pray You will bring about a change of heart. You said, that we should "…train up the child in the way he should go: and when he is old, he will not depart from it" (Proverbs 22:6).

    I'm afraid that without help this problem will get worse, Dear Lord, how can I motivate this youngster to take more of an interest in school? I want to do whatever I can; but I need Your wisdom. You said, "If any of you lack wisdom, let him ask of God, that giveth to all men liberally, and upbraideth not; and it shall be given him" (James 1:5). Your loving presence inspires me to try harder to make sure that school will be a happier time in this loved one's young life. AMEN

# He Will Hear

Father, You are my helper, put Your arm around my shoulder...and let us journey together. For I feel so safe here with You!

> The Lord is my light and my salvation; whom shall I fear? The Lord is the strength of my life; of whom shall I be afraid? Psalm 27:1

> The righteous cry, and the Lord heareth, and delivereth them out of all their troubles.
> Psalm 34:17

> But know that the Lord hath set apart him that is godly for himself: the Lord will hear when I call unto him. Psalm 4:3

> And this is the confidence that we have in him, that, if we ask anything according to his will he heareth us: and if we know that he hear us, whatsoever we ask, we know that we have the petitions that we desired of him. I John 5:14-15

> But let him ask in faith, nothing wavering. For he that wavereth is like a wave of the sea driven with the wind and tossed. James 1:6

# Deliver Me from My Leg Problems Take Away from Me All Sickness

You are my rock, Dear Father - You are my very foundation. How thankful I am for guidance and comfort which You have always given me in my life!

I pray that You will deliver me from my bad <u>leg problems.</u> Please guide me now to trust in You and in Your will...and to have faith in Your Word.

I am a member in the Body of Christ. I am redeemed from the curse, for Jesus bore my sickness and carried my diseases in His own body. (Galatians 3:13)

Satan, I rebuke you in the name of Jesus.

Father I pray that You will release the healing in my legs. I take authority over the muscles, tissues, and veins in the legs that they function the way You originally created them. The blood flows through my body and nourishes each cell which brings life instead of death. In the name of Jesus.

# Confession of Healing

1. You are the Lord that heals me. (Exodus 15:26)
2. You take sickness away from the midst of me and the number of my days you fulfill. (Exodus 23:25,26)
3. You take away from me all sickness. (Deuteronomy 7:15)
4. I am redeemed from the curse of the law. (Deuteronomy 28 & Galatians 3:13)
5. You heal all my diseases. (Psalms 103:3)
6. You sent your word and healed me and delivered me from my destruction. (Psalms 107:20)
7. I shall not die, but live, and declare the works of the Lord. (Psalms 91:16)
8. With long life you will satisfy me and show me your salvation. (Psalms 91:16)
9. Your words are life to me and health/medicine to all my flesh. (Proverbs 4:22)
10. Surely he hath borne my sicknesses and carried my pains. Himself took my infirmities and bare my sicknesses. (Isaiah 53:4)
11. With His stripes I am healed. (Isaiah 53:5) By His stripes I was healed. (I Peter 2:24)
12. The Life of Jesus is made manifest in my mortal body.
13. The same spirit that raised Christ up from the dead quickens my mortal body. (Romans 8:11)

14. Hands were laid on me and I am recovering. (Mark 16:18)
15. I call my body healed/whole. (Romans 4:17)

## I want to be Relieved from Arthritis

Father, I pray to You for relief from the arthritis with which I am now suffering. Dear Lord, please help me to hold on to the word I need to get me through these rough times. For You are the Lord that heals me (Exodus 15:26).

For the Word of God is quick, and powerful, and sharper than any two-edged sword, piercing even to the dividing asunder of soul and spirit, and of the joints and marrow, and is a discerner of the heart (Hebrews 4:12).

Thank You in the name of Jesus.

# Prayer for Overweight

I don't desire to eat so much that I become overweight. I present my body to You God. My body is the temple of the Holy Ghost, which dwells in me. I am not my own, I am bought with a price, therefore in the name of Jesus I refuse to overeat. Body, settle down in the name of Jesus and conform to the Word of God. I mortify the desires of this body and command it to come in to line with the Word of God.

Romans 12:1; I Corinthians 6:19

# Prayer for High Blood Pressure

Casting all your care upon Him. (I Peter 5:7)

Father, thou wilt keep him in perfect peace whose mind is stayed on thee, because he trusteth in thee. (Isaiah 26:3)

I suffer from high blood pressure O Lord, and when I am excited or worried, it gets worse. Stay with me, I pray and let Your warm and loving Spirit ease my mind when I feel upset. Grant me serenity and freedom from tension, day by day. Guide me to slow down when I should and to take it easy for my health sake.

Thank You, Father, for hearing my prayer, thank You for the peace I feel in my heart and my mind as I kneel before Your throne of grace. Truly, I know that the prayer of faith shall save the sick. In the name of Jesus.

# A Prayer for Deliverance from Lupus

    Father, I first would like to thank You for letting me even live to see another beautiful day. Father, I pray that You rid my body of any symptoms of "this" lupus. Nothing for You is impossible!

    I rebuke anymore joint stiffness, in the Name of Jesus! I rebuke anymore organ failures, in the Name of Jesus! I rebuke anymore unwelcomed hospital stays, in the Name of Jesus! I rebuke anymore rashes on my skin, in the Name of Jesus! I rebuke anymore hair loss, in the Name of Jesus!

    I expect for my body to function the way that You intended it to, for by Your stripes I am healed! The devil is a LIAR!!!! I receive and believe this blessing in Jesus' Holy name! Amen.

**Angelic Watkins**
*September, 2013*

# A Prayer for Deliverance from Sickle Cell Anemia

Dear Heavenly Father, the doctor may have diagnosed me with sickle cell disease; but I want to thank You for blessing me the knowledge I need to stave off some of the painful crises that occur with this condition. I praise You for providing the minerals of zinc and folic acid in earth's creation as powerful ways to acquire a healthy height and weight. I am thankful that these things help me to overcome the anemia that brings the awful tiredness that saps much needed energy.

Thank You Lord for giving me the wisdom to give my body the rest it needs, the self-control of the fruit of Your Spirit to live a life of moderation, with no smoking and hard drinking. Thank You for fresh clean water to drink to keep my body hydrated; especially when I feel mild pain and anemia.

I praise Your name for empowering me with the ability to stay away from a lot of junk food. Thank You for enabling me to eat more fruit and vegetables; and for the availability of good quality multivitamins to take with my meals.

I also thank You Lord for providing me with a good doctor and hematologist. I really appreciate the good relationship we have established as I keep all my appointments. Lastly Father, I want to thank You for all my family members who are prayer warriors. I know that You have been answering their prayers.

Thank You for using this prayer to open the eyes of others who may be struggling with this disease. May the stronghold of the devil be broken as in Christ we stand by faith. I pray this prayer of thanksgiving for all the things You are doing on our behalf, both seen and unseen. In Jesus' name, amen.

**Derrick Webb**
*October, 2013*

# A Prayer for Deliverance from Post Traumatic Stress Disorder
## (PTSD)

Lord, I am tired of my distress that I deal with from day to day. I need help from above. I need You to speak to me so, I can be free from my pain.

You are my Lord. You are my God. You see and You know my discomfort. Take away my shame, my pain, and my hurt that fills my soul each day.

I have fears that overtake me and I don't know how to handle them all. I believe that You will help me Lord. So this is my prayer to You. By faith I receive healing Heavenly Father. Amen.

LaTonia Dykes-Jones
*September, 2013*

# Praying the Word of God

Because whatsoever I ask in His name, that He will do, that the Father might be glorified in the Son. If I ask anything in His name, He will do it. I know that anything includes salvation, healing, supplying my needs, liberations and more. Therefore, I confidently speak in His name that the Father might be glorified. (John 14:13-14)

If I abide in Him, and His words abide in me I can ask what I will and it shall be done unto me. (John 15:7)

And it will come to pass that before I call Him, God will answer and while I am yet speaking He will hear me. (Isaiah 65:24)

I am of God and have overcome him (Satan). For greater is He that is in me, than he that is in the world. (I John 4:4)

I am far from oppression. And fear does not come nigh me. (Isaiah 54:14)

I take the shield of faith and I quench every fiery dart that wicked one brings against me. Because I am an overcomer and I overcome by the blood of the lamb and the word of my testimony. (Ephesians 6:16; Revelation 12:11)

I cast all my care upon Him because I know He cares for me. (I Peter 5:7)

Every sad depression filled valley of my life shall be exalted, and every hindrance and obstacles that blocks my way like a mountain or hill shall be brought down and made low: and the crooked perverse attempt against me shall be made straight and the rough places plain. (Isaiah 40:4)

The Lord has left His peace with me. His peace He gave to me. Not peace like the world gives grounded in false hopes, alcohol or illicit drugs. Therefore, I will not let my heart be troubled; neither will I let it be afraid. (John 14:27)

Lord, I will not fear for You are with me. I will not be dismayed; for You are my God: You will strengthen me, yes, You will help me; yes, You will uphold me with the right hand of Your righteousness. (Isaiah 41:10)

I am the body of Christ and Satan hath no power over me. For I overcome evil with good. (I Corinthians 12:27; Romans 12:21)

Hereby know I that the Spirit of God; every spirit that confesses that Jesus Christ is come in the flesh is of God. And every spirit that confesses not that Jesus Christ is come in the flesh is not of God. Since I confess that Jesus is the son of God, God dwells in me and me in God. (I John 4:2-3, 15)

"I have been young, and now am old; yet have I not seen the righteous forsaken, nor his seed begging bread." (Psalm 37:25)

Though I may go forth weeping as I bear my precious seed, there is no doubt that I will come again with rejoicing bringing my sheaves with me. (Psalm 126:6)

I have put off the old man and have put on the new man which is renewed in knowledge after the image of Him that created me. (Colossians 3:10)

I am born of God and I have world overcoming faith residing on the inside of me. For greater is He that is in me, that he that is in the world. (I John 5:4-5; I John 4:4)

And it shall come to pass that because I have called upon the name of the Lord that I shall be saved. (Acts 2:21)

I take authority over the words of my mouth and the meditation of my heart so, that they are acceptable in the sight of my Lord, my strength, and my redeemer. (Psalm 19:14)

I am filled with the knowledge of the Lord's will in all wisdom and spiritual understanding. (Colossians 1:9)

I put my trust in the Lord. Therefore, I shall be made fat on the goodness of the Lord. (Proverbs 28:25)

When I receive the riches of God's blessing I can rejoice because His blessing makes rich and adds no sorrow with it. (Proverbs 10:22)

I am the body of Christ and Satan hath no power over me. For I overcome evil with good. (I Corinthians 12:27; Romans 12:21)

I will fear no evil for thou art with me Lord, your Word and your Spirit they comfort me. (Psalms 23:4).

I am far from oppression, and fear does not come nigh me. (Isaiah 54:14)

Because Jesus, the Son of Man, came to seek and to save that which was lost, I am found. Now I am free to minister to others. After I received the power of the Holy Ghost upon me I was empowered to go and teach all nations, baptizing them in the name of the Father and of the Son, and of the Holy Ghost. (Luke 19:10; Acts 1:8; Matthew 28:19)

No weapon formed against me shall prosper, for my righteousness is of the Lord. But whatever I do will prosper for I'm like a tree that's planted by the rivers of water. (Isaiah 54:17; Psalms 1:3)

No evil will befall thee neither shall any plague come nigh my dwelling. For the Lord has given his angels charge over me and they keep me in all my ways, and in my path way is life and there is no death. (Psalms 91:10-11; Proverbs 12:28)

Christ has redeemed me from the curse of the law. Therefore, I forbid any sickness or disease to come upon this body. Every disease germ and every virus that touches this body dies instantly in the Name of Jesus. Every organ and every tissue of this body functions in the perfection to which God created it to function, and I forbid any malfunction in this body, in the Name of Jesus. (Galatians 3:13; Romans 8:11; Genesis 1:31; Matthew 16:19)

For poverty he has given me wealth, for sickness he has given me health, for death he has given me eternal life: (II Corinthians 8:9; Isaiah 53:5-6).

Great is the peace of my children for they are taught of the Lord. (Isaiah 54:13)

I take the shield of faith and I quench every fiery dart that the wicked one brings against me. (Ephesians 6:16)

I am an overcomer and I overcome by the blood of the lamb and the word of my testimony. (Revelation 12:11)

I am submitted to God and the devil flees from me because I resist him in the Name of Jesus. (James 4:7)

The Word of God is forever settled in heaven. Therefore, I establish His Word upon this earth. (Psalms 119:89)

The weapons of my warfare are not carnal; but they are mighty through God to the pulling down of strongholds. Therefore, I submit myself to God and I resist the devil and he flees from me. (II Corinthians 11:4; James 4:7)

As one beloved of God I am determined to be steadfast, unmoveable, always abounding in the work of the Lord. For I know that my labor is not in vain in the Lord. (I Corinthians 15:58)

# What are the Signs of the End?

And Jesus answered and said unto them, Take heed that no man deceive you. For many shall come in my name saying I am Christ; and shall deceive many. And ye shall hear of wars and rumors of wars: see that ye be not troubled: for all these things must come to pass, but the end is not yet. For nation shall rise against nation, and kingdom against kingdom: and there shall be famines, and pestilence, and earthquakes in divers places. All these are the beginning of sorrows.

This know also, that in the last days perilous times shall come. For men shall be lovers of their own selves, covetous, boasters, proud, blasphemers, disobedient to parents, unthankful, unholy, without natural affection, trucebreakers, false accusers, incontinent, fierce despisers of those that are good. And it shall come to pass in the last days, saith God, I will pour out of my spirit upon all flesh: and your sons and your daughters shall prophesy, and your young men shall see visions, and your old men shall dream dreams: but, beloved, be not ignorant of this one thing, that one day is with the Lord as a thousand years, and a thousand years as one day.

Keep yourselves in the love of God, looking for the mercy of our Lord Jesus Christ unto eternal life in His name. Amen.
II Timothy 1:1-3; Acts 2:17; II Peter 3:8; Jude 21

# About the Author
## Evangelist Ivy Caddell

Evangelist Ivy Caddell is a *"Faith Warrior"* in and for the Lord's purpose in her life. She is a native of Tuscaloosa, Alabama and was educated at the Tuscaloosa State Trade School where she received her education in cosmetology. She continued her education and received degrees from Cleary College (Fashion Merchandising), Aenon Bible College (Ministerial License) and Ann Arbor Institute of Massage Therapy (Certification in Massage Therapy), when she moved to Ypsilanti, Michigan.

She is the owner of the *Health and Wellness Day Spa* and *Hats by IvyMar*. She also hosts a Healing School Conference Line. Ivy holds many titles: Northern District Council Evangelist Chairperson, Author, Massage Therapist, Herbalist and founder of *With God All Things Are Possible Ministries*.

Coming from circumstances in life that would astound many, she has let God's word live within her to be made whole. Evangelist Caddell believes in speaking, teaching, walking and talking the Word of God! She has been in ministry since 1983, and involved as an Altar Worker. She leads the Prayer Ministry at Messias Temple Church, Ypsilanti, Michigan, currently under the pastorate of Bishop Harry S. Grayson, where she has been a member since 1979.

Ivy is a lover of life and people. She is the wife of the late Trustee Tom Caddell, Jr.; the mother of LaTonia Dykes-Jones; the grandmother of two grandsons; and great-grandmother of one great-granddaughter.

Evangelist Caddell believes that the *"ANOINTING DESTROYS THE YOKE and REMOVES IT!"*

> *And if we know that He hears us, whatsoever we ask, we know that we have the petitions that we desired of Him.*
>
> I John 5:15

So, if we are praying GOD'S WORD, then we know He hears us and our prayers are being answered because Heaven and Earth shall pass away before HIS WORD does! Let's celebrate the Power and the Glory that is within *us-BELIEVE ON THE **LORD**, as you pray "Prayers for Daily Strength!"*

*For more information or to contact Evangelist Caddell visit:*

*Email: info@IvyCaddell.com*
*Website: www.IvyCaddell.com*

# *Prayers for Daily Strength*

## Praying the Answer NOT the Problem
### By Ivy Caddell

**Name** _____

**Address** _____

**City** _____ **State** _____ **Zip** _____

**Phone** _____ **Fax** _____

**Email** _____

| Quantity | |
|---|---|
| Price *(each)* | $12.99 |
| Subtotal | |
| S & H | $1.99 |
| Additional copies | |
| **TOTAL** | |

*Add $0.75 shipping for each additional copy.*

**METHOD OF PAYMENT:**
❏ Check or Money Order (***Make payable to***: **Ivy Caddell**)

❏ Visa ❏ Master Card ❏ American Express
Acct No. _____ CVV _____

Expiration Date *(mmyy)* _____

Signature _____

***Mail your payment with this form to:***
Evangelist Ivy Caddell
866 Madison Street
Ypsilanti, MI 48197

Or feel free to order online at www.IvyCaddell.com

www.ingramcontent.com/pod-product-compliance
Lightning Source LLC
Chambersburg PA
CBHW052044070526
44584CB00018B/2607